DK READERS

Level 4

A Note to Parents

DK READERS is a compelling program for beginning readers, designed in conjunction with leading literacy experts.

Beautiful illustrations and superb full-color photographs combine with engaging, easy-to-read stories to offer a fresh approach to each subject in the series. Each DK READER is guaranteed to capture a child's interest while developing his or her reading skills, general knowledge, and love of reading.

The four levels of DK READERS are aimed at different reading abilities, enabling you to choose the books that are exactly right for your child:

Level 1 – Beginning to read
Level 2 – Beginning to read alone
Level 3 – Reading alone
Level 4 – Proficient readers

The "normal" age at which a child begins to read can be anywhere from three to eight years old, so these levels are only a general guideline.

No matter which level you select, you can be sure that you are helping your child learn to read, then read to learn!

LONDON, NEW YORK, DELHI,
MUNICH, AND MELBOURNE

Created by Tall Tree Ltd

Editor Jon Richards
Designer Ed Simkins

For DK
Series Editor Alastair Dougall
Series Designer Rob Perry
Production Nicola Torode
Picture Researcher Harriet Mills
Picture Library Sarah Mills

Cover art by Adam Hughes

First American Edition, 2004

Published in the United States by
DK Publishing, Inc.
375 Hudson Street
New York, New York 10014

04 05 06 07 08 10 9 8 7 6 5 4 3 2 1

Page design copyright © 2004 Dorling Kindersley Limited

A Cataloging-in-Publication record for this book
is available from the Library of Congress.

ISBN 0-7566-0242-4

Color reproduction by Media Development and Printing Ltd, UK
Printed and bound in China by L Rex Printing Co., Ltd.

The publisher thanks the following for their kind permission
to reproduce their photographs:
(Key: a=above; c=center; b=below; l=left; r=right; t=top)
AKG London: Andrea Baguzzi 10-11; The Art Archive: Musée du Louvre
Paris / Dagli Orti 19l; Corbis: Vanni Archive 9br; Roger Wood 45c; DK
Images: British Museum 13tr, 16-17, 28-29, 34-35, 36-37, 39t; Barnabas
Kindersley 40b, 43b; Judith Miller/Albert Amor UK 6-7; Judith
Miller/Lyon & Turnbull 23bl; TAP 13b, 21b; Getty Images: Peter Gridley
46-47; Mary Evans Picture Library: 31bl; Edwin Wallace 33l.

All other photographs © Dorling Kindersley www.dkimages.com

Dorling Kindersley would like to thank the following artists:
Shawn Atkinson, Michael Bair, Eric Battle, Rick Burchett, Sal Buscema,
John Byrne, James Calafiore, Matthew Clark, Mike Deodato, Drew Geraci,
Dick Giordano, Mick Gray, Phil Jimenez, Barry Kitson, Andy Lanning,
Jim Lee, Doug Mahnke, Alitha Martinez, Ray McCarthy, Ed McGuinness,
Mark McKenna, Bob McLeod, Lan Medina, Tom Nguyen, Yanick Paquette,
Ande Parks, Bruce Patterson, George Pérez, Howard Porter, Tom Simmons,
Cam Smith, Tim Truman, and Walden Wong.

Dorling Kindersley would also like to thank the following:
Scott Beatty, Ivan Cohen, and Phil Jiminez.

Discover more at
www.dk.com

Contents

 READERS

JLA WONDER WOMAN'S BOOK OF
MYTHS

Written by Clare Hibbert
Wonder Woman created by
William Moulton Marston

Wonder Woman's super strength comes from Gaea, the Earth goddess. Gaea even had a hand in creating the Amazons. They were made from souls she had saved.

The souls of the Amazons were cast into a lake in ancient Greece, from which they emerged as a race of human women. Wonder Woman was raised as a princess of this special group.

Amazonian princess

Myths are cool stories about gods and super-heroes—like me! They feature fantastic battles, mind-boggling adventures, and big ideas, such as the struggle between good and evil. I'm going to introduce you to some amazing myths that were first told thousands of years ago. Maybe it's not surprising that many of my favorites come from the ancient Greeks, who lived in southern Europe nearly three thousand years ago. The ancient Greeks told tales of a race of warrior women called the Amazons, who were ruled by a queen named Hippolyta. And, as you know, I am Hippolyta's daughter, which makes me princess of the Amazons.

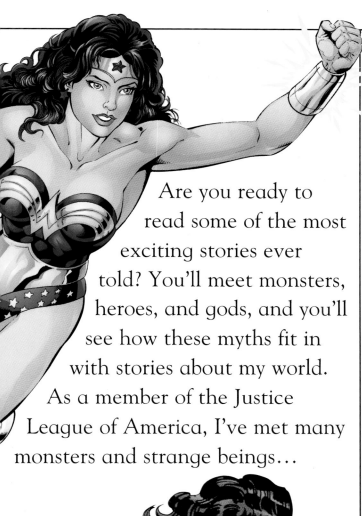

Are you ready to read some of the most exciting stories ever told? You'll meet monsters, heroes, and gods, and you'll see how these myths fit in with stories about my world. As a member of the Justice League of America, I've met many monsters and strange beings…

Wonder Woman is a key member of the Justice League of America, the JLA, along with other superheroes such as Superman, Batman, and the Flash.

Hippolyta's helper
The god Hermes helped the Amazonian queen to create her daughter. Hippolyta made a clay figure and the god breathed life into it.

King of the gods

All the gods in Greek myth were ruled by Zeus—though he was lucky to be alive! Zeus' father was Chronos, king of a race of giants called the Titans. Chronos had been told that one day his own son would overthrow him. Each time his wife Rhea had a child, Chronos ate it.

When Rhea gave birth to Zeus, she tricked Chronos into eating a stone wrapped in blankets. Zeus was raised in secret— and eventually went on to overthrow his father.

King of the superheroes
Just as Zeus rules over the Olympian gods, Superman heads the Justice League of America. All the other superheroes respect him as the team's leader.

Zeus' wife Hera was often jealous about her husband's affairs with mortal women. She even tried to kill some of his lovers and the children his affairs produced.

The ancient Greeks worshiped Zeus as king of the gods. They built many temples and statues in his honor.

Zeus became king of the gods, and shared control of the entire cosmos with his brothers, Poseidon and Hades. Poseidon took charge of the seas and oceans, while Hades controlled the kingdom of the dead, called the Underworld, and Zeus ruled the sky.

Zeus had a reputation as a ladies' man. He had at least three wives, the last of whom was Hera, as well as a great many love affairs—with mortal women as well as goddesses.

Bracelets
Wonder Woman's bulletproof bracelets were created from the remains of Zeus' magic shield, known as the Aegis.

Royal favor
The goddess Athena asked Hephaestus to make the bracelets, as a prize for the worthiest Amazon.

This statue of Zeus shows him flanked by two majestic eagles—symbols of his power.

7

Wonder Woman went to live on Olympus for a short time as the goddess of truth.

Splitting gods
In Wonder Woman's universe, Uxas split the gods in two, creating the Roman gods. Hermes was split to form Mercury, his Roman version.

Mount Olympus

The gods and goddesses ruled by Zeus make up the Greek pantheon, or collection of gods. They are also sometimes called the Olympians, after Mount Olympus. At nearly 10,000 feet (3,000 meters) above sea level, Mount Olympus is the highest mountain in Greece.

The Greeks believed that the gods lived high on the mountain's peak, where they had a wonderful view of all of Greece.

The Olympians did not always behave in a very godlike manner. They spent a lot of their time quarreling, playing tricks on each other, or even taking revenge!

Even after ancient Greece was conquered by the Romans, stories of the Olympians lived on. The Romans adopted the Greek gods, but changed many of their names.

New Olympus
One of Wonder Woman's worst enemies is Darkseid, the ruler of Apokolips. After he destroyed Mount Olympus, the Olympian gods had to make a new home floating in the clouds, which they called New Olympus.

Zeus, for example, changed his name to become the Roman sky-god, Jupiter.

Mount Olympus stands high above the rest of Greece and is always covered in snow.

God of war

The terrifying Greek god of war was called Ares. Just the sound of his battle cry could kill a mortal!

The Greeks believed there were noble aspects to warfare, but Ares stood for the bloodthirsty, brutal side of it. Even Zeus, Ares' own father, called him the "most hateful of gods."

Most of the Olympians disliked Ares because of his temper.

Home on a hill
The home of the god of war was called the Areopagus, which is Greek for "Hill of Ares."

Deadly enemy
Wonder Woman was created to defeat Ares. In doing so, she stopped him from starting World War III and a nuclear holocaust.

However, Aphrodite, the goddess of love, had an affair with him, and gave birth to their son, the cherub Eros. One shot from his bow and arrow could make someone fall hopelessly in love!

Eros was just a mischief-maker, but most of Ares' sons were evil. They included Phobos, meaning "fear," Deimos, meaning "terror," and Kyknos, who tried to build a temple out of skulls. Another of Ares' offspring was a terrible dragon. After it was killed, warriors sprang up where its teeth had fallen.

Ari Buchanan
At one time, Ares inhabited the body of a petty criminal named Ari Buchanan and turned him into a Boston crime lord.

Areopagus
The children of Ares wanted to take over Gotham City and rename it Areopagus. Batman foiled their plans, with help from Wonder Woman, Troia, Wonder Girl, and Artemis.

Ares stands ready for battle. He wears chest armor and a plumed helmet, and carries a round shield.

Hera and Hestia

Two of the most important goddesses on Olympus were Hera and Hestia.

Hera was the goddess of women, marriage, and childbirth. Most importantly, she was married to Zeus, and this made her the queen of all the gods in Olympus.

However, their marriage was far from happy. Zeus was always making Hera jealous by falling in love with other women. When she was not quarreling with her husband or trying to catch him having affairs, Hera was usually plotting revenge on the many rivals she had for her husband's love.

Hestia was a wise old goddess—far too wise to get involved with men! She refused offers of marriage from Apollo and Poseidon.

Gift from a goddess
Hestia gave Wonder Woman her magical Lasso of Truth. Anyone bound in its loop has no choice but to tell the truth.

Wonder Woman never misses when she throws her golden lasso.

Zeus was so taken with Hestia's wisdom that he made her the goddess in charge of festivals. She was also goddess of families and of the hearth.

Child killer
Hera was jealous of Heracles, Zeus' son by another woman. She sent a pair of snakes to kill him in his cradle. Luckily, Heracles was strong even then. He strangled the snakes with his bare hands!

Clay head showing the face of the goddess Hera.

© TAP

13

Hermes

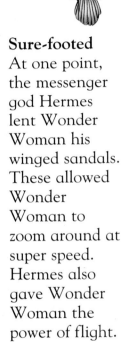

Hermes, known to the Romans as Mercury, was the messenger of the gods. He had a pair of golden, winged sandals that helped him to whiz around from place to place.

Sure-footed
At one point, the messenger god Hermes lent Wonder Woman his winged sandals. These allowed Wonder Woman to zoom around at super speed. Hermes also gave Wonder Woman the power of flight.

Hermes' parents were Zeus and a beautiful nymph named Maia. Even as a baby, Hermes was adventurous—and loved making mischief. He escaped from his cradle and played a trick on the god Apollo by hiding a herd of his cattle. When Apollo confronted him, Hermes made a peace offering.

Hermes wore wings on his sandals and his traveling hat. He carried a herald's (or messenger's) staff, called a kerykeion.

He gave Apollo a musical instrument he had invented, called the lyre. It was a tortoise shell with strings across it, which had been made from the gut of one of Apollo's cattle.

Hermes became the god of herds, business, travelers, and thieves, and he was responsible for guiding the souls of the dead down to the Underworld. Hermes was also the god of dreams and it was traditional for the ancient Greeks to offer their last drink of the evening to him so that he would grant them a restful night's sleep.

Flash
The Justice League of America's speedster is the Flash. He became a super-hero after he was hit by a thunderbolt.

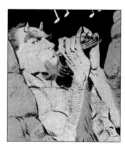

In Wonder Woman's universe, Hermes' son was a satyr named Pan. Pan was killed and replaced by an android, but Wonder Woman destroyed the robot replacement.

Heracles, urged on by Ares, managed to defeat the Amazons by trickery and enslave them.

Hidden hero
Wonder Woman fell in love with Heracles while he was in disguise as the super hero Champion.

Heracles

Many myths are about heroes with superhuman powers. Heracles, or Hercules to the Romans, was the greatest of them all. His father was great Zeus himself and his mother was a mortal named Alcmene.

Heracles is most famous for his Twelve Labors, a set of nearly impossible tasks. These involved killing fearsome beasts, such as a man-eating lion, the nine-headed Hydra, a flock of savage birds, and the dragon that guarded golden apples belonging to Hera.

He also wrestled a fierce bull and kidnapped some flesh-eating horses. He even overpowered Cerberus, the three-headed hound that stood guard at the gates of hell.

By completing the Twelve Labors, Heracles proved his godlike strength and bravery.

Some years after he finished the last of these, Heracles was poisoned, but only the mortal part of him died. The rest of him went to join the gods and goddesses on Mount Olympus, and he became one of the immortals.

Reminder
The Amazons managed to free themselves from slavery under Heracles by praying to Athena. But Hippolyta, Wonder Woman's mother, still wears the Bracelets of Submission to mark her defeat by Heracles.

© British Museum

Heracles killing a flock of savage birds, one of his Twelve Labors.

Athena

Athena was the Greek goddess of war and wisdom. Her father was Zeus and her mother was Metis, one of the Titans. Zeus had swallowed Metis in case their child overthrew him, just as he had overthrown his own father. But Athena was born, unharmed, from her father's head. Tall, regal, and dressed in fine armor, she quickly became Zeus' favorite child.

The city of Athens was named after Athena, and she was its patron goddess. The Athenians built a temple in her honor, the Parthenon. Inside stood an ivory and gold statue of Athena holding Nike, goddess of victory.

Although Athena was usually merciful, she was still a war goddess. During the Trojan Wars, Athena gave advice to the Greeks.

Battle armor
Wonder Woman's ceremonial gold armor with wings was made by Athena herself. The goddess also gave Wonder Woman the gift of wisdom.

Athena, dressed for battle with a plumed helmet and spear. Flying next to her is the owl that was her mascot and the symbol of Athens.

Wisdom of Athena
Members of the Justice League of America know just who to turn to for wise advice. The JLA coordinator Oracle is a kind of online help resource!

She helped one of the Greek leaders, Odysseus, come up with the idea of building a wooden horse to trick the Trojans. By hiding inside the horse, the Greeks were able to sneak into Troy itself.

Aphrodite

The goddess Aphrodite wore a magic girdle that could make any man fall in love with her.

Although she married Hephaestus, the lame god of metalworking, she had no intention of staying faithful to him. She was the goddess of love, after all! Aphrodite had love affairs with the gods Ares, Hermes, and Dionysus, as well as mortals such as handsome Adonis.

One day, Aphrodite found herself at a wedding. Eris, goddess of discord, had brought along a golden apple inscribed "For the most beautiful." Aphrodite thought that must mean her, but Hera and Athena each thought that *they* were the most beautiful!

Paris, a prince from the city of Troy, had to judge, and he chose Aphrodite as the most beautiful.

Love and beauty
Aphrodite gave Wonder Woman the gifts of great beauty and a loving heart.

Forging ahead
Aphrodite was married to Hephaestus. The lame god forged Wonder Woman's magic bracelets and her lasso.

In return, she helped him to run off with Helen, the King of Sparta's wife, starting the Trojan War. This was not the only time that Aphrodite's meddling got men into trouble.

Steel
JLA member Steel knows a thing or two about metalworking. He has his own foundry in his HQ, the SteelWorks. This is where he makes his body armor.

As well as being the goddess of love, Aphrodite was worshiped as the goddess of the sea.

21

Demeter

Creating souls
Demeter was one of the five goddesses who helped to create the Amazons using souls saved by Gaea.

The five goddesses selected the spirits of the Amazons from the Well of Souls, a dark region where the spirits of humans circled aimlessly for hundreds of years.

Demeter was the Greek goddess of harvests and corn. She had a lovely young daughter named Persephone. One day, while Persephone was picking flowers, the ground opened and swallowed her up. Hades, the god who ruled the Underworld, had kidnapped her!

Demeter found out what had happened, and she swore that no corn would grow until Hades had returned Persephone to the surface.

Before too long, humankind was in danger of starving. Zeus asked Hades to return Persephone and Hades agreed, but with one condition. If any food from the Underworld passed Persephone's lips, she would not be allowed to leave.

Unfortunately, poor Persephone had eaten one tiny pomegranate seed while she had been kidnapped. After some thought, Hades agreed to allow Persephone to visit the Earth for eight months each year, on condition that she spend four months with him down in the Underworld.

Gaea's gift
Demeter gave Wonder Woman her super strength. The goddess was able to do this through a connection with Gaea, or Mother Earth.

The ancient Greeks believed that winter happened when Demeter (right) was missing her daughter Persephone (left).

Hades

If you were an ancient Greek, the Underworld was your idea of hell— and heaven! Good or bad, all souls went there after death. It was ruled by Hades, the god of the dead.

To reach the Underworld, the dead were ferried across the River Styx. Then they crossed the Plain of Asphodel and the Meadows of Erebus. If they stopped to drink at the River Lethe, they forgot all about their past life.

Hades appointed three judges to decide which path a soul must take next. The first path led back to the Plain of Asphodel. Here, souls wandered forever in the misty twilight.

Afterlife
Artemis is an Amazon warrior who lived in the Underworld for a time after she was killed by the White Magician. Fortunately, Wonder Woman rescued Artemis from Dälkrij-Hath, Prince of Hades.

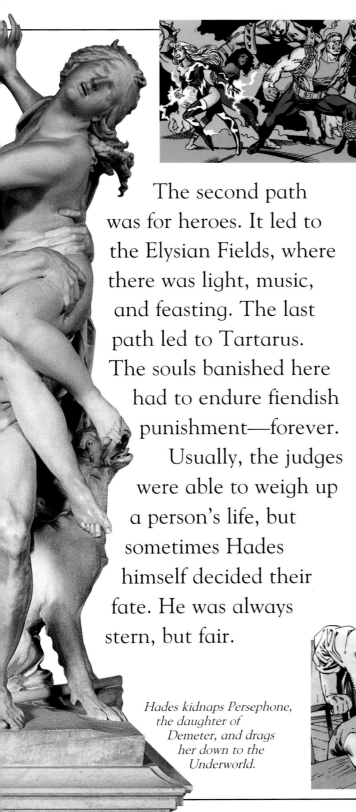

The second path was for heroes. It led to the Elysian Fields, where there was light, music, and feasting. The last path led to Tartarus. The souls banished here had to endure fiendish punishment—forever.

Usually, the judges were able to weigh up a person's life, but sometimes Hades himself decided their fate. He was always stern, but fair.

Hades kidnaps Persephone, the daughter of Demeter, and drags her down to the Underworld.

After her rescue, Artemis joined the Hellenders and changed her name to Requiem.

Desperate drug
Lethe, a vile creature from Tartarus, made a powerful drug that Wendy Mayer became addicted to. Wonder Woman and her friend, the policeman Ed Indelicato, saved her from this addiction.

Artemis and Apollo

Artemis was the Greek goddess of hunting and nature, and she carried a bow with silver arrows. Followed by a band of nymphs, she drove her chariot through fields and woods, hunting deer and wild boar.

Artemis' twin brother was Apollo, the god of light. Their parents were Zeus and a Titan named Leto. Zeus' jealous wife Hera sent a giant serpent called the Python after Leto. Later in life, Apollo shot down the Python to avenge his mother. He also killed the one-eyed Cyclopes.

Amazonian worship
Artemis is the chief goddess worshiped by the Amazons. They honor the goddess by sacrificing a deer in her name.

The Amazon Artemis is highly skilled with a bow and arrow.

For this act, he spent a year in exile in Tartarus.

Eventually, Apollo grew calmer. He became god of healing, the arts, and music. No one could match his singing or lyre-playing. But although he was gifted and handsome, Apollo was unlucky in love. After his lover Coronis cheated on him, Artemis killed her with an arrow.

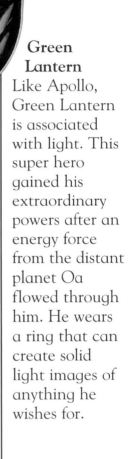

Green Lantern
Like Apollo, Green Lantern is associated with light. This super hero gained his extraordinary powers after an energy force from the distant planet Oa flowed through him. He wears a ring that can create solid light images of anything he wishes for.

As the god of light, Apollo was supposed to pull the sun across the sky each day using his chariot.

Ruler of the waves

Zeus' brother Poseidon was lord of the oceans and all marine creatures. He drove a chariot pulled by golden seahorses, and his palace was decorated with coral and shells.

Despite his vast kingdom, Poseidon was unhappy. He once tried to claim Athens, even though it was the realm of his niece, Athena.

Poseidon was a very bad-tempered god. He used a large, forked weapon called a trident to stir up fierce storms. By banging it on the sea floor, he caused terrible earthquakes.

Poseidon founded the legendary island of Atlantis and fathered its first people. Later, the Atlantians became wicked and greedy, so Poseidon was forced to destroy the kingdom.

Aquaman
JLA member Aquaman can communicate telepathically with all forms of sea life. He often has run-ins with Poseidon and his son, Triton.

Aquaman took his rightful place as King of Atlantis, but later he had to sink the ancient city. He did this to rescue his people from their magical ancestors.

He battered it with earthquakes and tidal waves.

The sea god fathered some strange children. One son, Triton, was half man, half fish. Poseidon was also the father of Pegasus, a flying horse, and Polyphemus, a one-eyed giant.

Saved from the sea
As a baby, Julia Kapatelis fell off her parents' fishing boat. She was saved from drowning by sea nymphs called the Nereides, who washed her ashore on the island of Themyscira. Julia went on to become a close friend of Wonder Woman.

A dish showing the head of the sea god in the center, surrounded by the sea nymphs known as the Nereides.

The Titans

Greek myths tell of a time of nothingness, before any of the gods existed. Mother Earth, or Gaea, emerged from the chaos, and her son, Uranus, made the Earth.

Uranus and Gaea had six sons and six daughters. These were the Titans. When they grew up, they turned against their father. Chronos, the youngest of the Titans, killed Uranus and became ruler of the Titans.

Later, Chronos' own son, Zeus, turned against his father. Zeus gave Chronos a magic potion that made him sick. Out of his mouth came Hades, Poseidon, Demeter, Hera, and Hestia. These were Zeus' brothers and sisters—whom Chronos had swallowed as babies!

The gods wanted to punish the Titans for the pain they had caused.

Horrid Harrier
Harrier, one of the Titan monsters, was Chronus' son and one of Wonder Woman's most sinister foes. He had large wings and a serpent's tail, and was able to fly very quickly.

After ten years of bitter warfare, the gods won, and they banished the Titans to the Underworld. All except for Atlas, who had led the

Titan army—the gods had a special punishment for him.

Heaven's gate
In Wonder Woman's universe, all of the Titans, except for Chronus, were banished to a distant planet. Chronus believed that he should be the supreme power in the Universe, and he used his sickle to smash down the gates of heaven.

For his part in leading the Titans against the gods, Atlas was condemned to hold the entire weight of the heavens on his shoulders forever.

Evil sorceress Wonder Woman first met Circe when she was visiting Greece. But this character is not as helpful as her mythical namesake. Instead, she is a ruthless villain who tried to turn Diana back into clay.

Circe

Circe was a beautiful sorceress, daughter of the sun-god and a sea nymph. After she poisoned her husband, Circe was banished to the island of Aeaea. Here, she lived in a marble palace and practiced her magic. If anyone landed on her island, she used drugs and spells to change them into wild animals, and kept them as her servants.

One day, the hero Odysseus arrived at Aeaea—and Circe changed his sailors into pigs. On his way to rescue the men, Odysseus met the messenger-god Hermes. Hermes gave Odysseus a magic herb to protect him against Circe's magic. Odysseus forced Circe to change his men back into human form. The sorceress fell in love with him and persuaded him to stay with her for a year.

When Odysseus finally left Circe's island, the sorceress gave him lots of useful advice. Without her help, Odysseus would probably never have seen his homeland ever again.

Injustice Gang Circe is one of Wonder Woman's fiercest foes. She is an important member of the Injustice Gang, which also includes Lex Luthor and the Joker. They are the sworn enemies of the Justice League of America.

Odysseus' men stumbled across Circe's home when they were searching for food. They did not expect to end up as pigs!

Zeus made Diana fight the Minotaur, who proved to be no match for Wonder Woman.

Challenge of the Gods
After Wonder Woman rejected Zeus' advances, he forced her to prove herself. He challenged her to fight the Chimera and she won, with a little help from Hippolyta.

Terrible monsters

Greek myths are full of the most horrible monsters, many of which were hybrids—mixes of different creatures. The Minotaur was half man, half bull and lived in a labyrinth, or maze. Each year it gobbled up 14 young people—until the hero Theseus killed it. The fire-breathing Chimera was half lion and half goat, with a serpent for a tail. Prince Bellerophon destroyed the Chimera by sticking lead-tipped spears into the monster's fiery mouth.

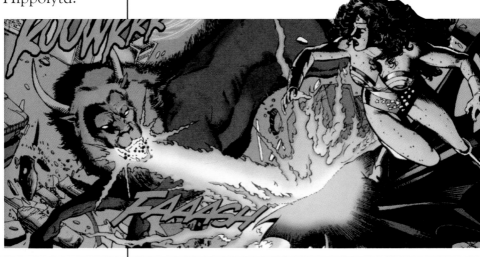

© British Museum

The Cheetah
Sébastian Ballesteros is a hybrid monster— half man, half cheetah. He makes a formidable foe for Wonder Woman, with his grasping tail and razor-sharp claws.

The lead melted and dribbled down the Chimera's throat, scorching it. The Chimera's parents were the 100-headed Typhon and Echidna, who was half woman and half snake.

Three of Greek myth's most horrible female monsters were sisters—Medusa, Sthenno, and Euryale—known as the Gorgons. They had scaly bodies, snakes for hair, and a gaze that could turn people to stone.

The Gorgons were immortals, but Medusa gave up her immortality. She was later killed by the hero Perseus. Even after he had cut off her head, her eyes kept their deadly gaze. Perseus used Medusa's head as a weapon to turn some of his enemies into stone statues.

The Hekatonchires were giants that had 50 heads and 100 arms. They lived in the Underworld and they were the children of Uranus and Gaea. Their brothers, the Cyclopes, also lived in the Underworld. Each had a single eye in the middle of its forehead. The Cyclopes helped Zeus in his fight against the Titans.

Another group of creepy creatures were the terrible Harpies, who had birds' bodies and women's heads. A group of Greek heroes named the Argonauts fought with the Harpies, as well as fire-breathing bulls and a dragon. These battles took place during their quest for the Golden Fleece, the skin of a flying golden ram.

Stony gaze
The Amazon warrior Nu'Bia made a pact with the Gorgons. As a result, her gaze turns other human beings into statues.

During his travels, Odysseus came across one of the Cyclopes, who took his men prisoner. Odysseus freed his men by blinding the one-eyed monster.

37

Friendly beasts

Not all mythological beasts were vicious monsters. Some were friendly, and they often helped heroes to defeat their enemies.

Pegasus was a winged horse that sprang from the blood of Medusa when she was killed. Pegasus could fly through the air, and he allowed the prince Bellerophon to ride him when he fought the fire-breathing Chimera.

Centaurs were half human and half horse, and they could be savage, but also very wise.

Sphinx and Pegasus moved into the WonderDome, Wonder Woman's magical old base.

Caring centaur
The centaur Chiron cared for Wonder Woman when she was injured in battle.

© British Museum

Evil centaur
While true centaurs are good, Chronus' son Slaughter was definitely evil. He had a deadly weapon at the end of each arm and clashed with Wonder Woman more than once.

The wisest of the centaurs was Chiron. Many of the great Greek heroes, including Heracles, Achilles, and Jason, were taught by Chiron. After Heracles accidentally shot him with a poisoned arrow, the centaur gave up his immortality.
He did not want to suffer the pain of the wound for eternity. Zeus placed Chiron among the stars, where he became the constellation Sagittarius.

Hindu gods

Some stories still form part of living religions, such as Hinduism. The main trinity, or Trimurti, of Hindu gods are Brahma, Siva, and Vishnu.

Hindu heaven
In Wonder Woman's universe, the Hindu gods live on Mount Mandara, a place that exists in many dimensions. The gods there inhabit many different levels of gravity, size, and space.

Ganesh is usually pictured red and with one of his tusks broken.

Brahma creates the universe at the beginning of each cycle of time. Siva destroys the universe at the end of each cycle.

The Hindu pantheon also includes hundreds of minor deities. Some are associated with animals. Hanuman is the monkey god. He helped the hero Rama to defeat the demon king Ravana. Ganesh, the god of good luck, has the head of an elephant. His brother is Skanda, the six-headed war god who rides a giant peacock.

Many Hindu goddesses are forms of one great goddess, called Mahadevi. In her warrior form, she produced the destroyer goddess Kali, who wore a necklace of human skulls. Kali helped her mother to defeat the demon Raktabija.

Hindu hell
The Rakshasas were demons that Wonder Woman defeated with the help of Nu'Bia, Artemis, and Shim'Tar.

Siva
The Hindu god Siva helped Ares, Loki, Mars, Huitzilpochtli, and Darkseid end the War of the Gods.

41

Earth savior
Wonder Woman was introduced to the Trimurti by an avatar of Vishnu who had been sent to save Earth.

Spiderwoman
Rama took the form of the goddess Kali to help Wonder Woman kill a spider monster created by Dr. Poison.

Avatars of Vishnu

Vishnu is the Hindu preserver-god who steadies the universe and protects humankind. If evil seems about to take control, Vishnu appears on Earth to restore the balance. He appears in different forms, which are called avatars. Ten of Vishnu's avatars are especially important.

These include the fish avatar, Matsya, who saved the first man during the Flood, and the tortoise avatar, Kurma, who propped the holy mountain Mandara on its back.

The avatars in human form included Krishna, who is now worshiped as a god, and the Buddha, the founder of Buddhism.

Vishnu's seventh avatar was the hero Rama. His story is written down in an epic poem called the *Ramayana*. Rama defeated the ten-headed demon king Ravana and his demon servants, the rakshasas, after they kidnapped his wife Sita.

Seeking help
Rama sought out Wonder Woman's help when he discovered that Chronus wanted to destroy Brahma, Siva, and Vishnu.

Vishnu is often pictured riding on the back of a golden peacock.

Mammitu is a goddess of the Underworld and is worshiped by the Bana-Mighdall Amazons.

Other Amazons
The tribe of Bana-Mighdall Amazons lived in Egypt. Wonder Woman first encountered them when she was chasing the Cheetah.

Egyptian deities

The ancient Egyptians had their own mythical stories. They believed that the sun-god, Re, traveled across the sky each day in his flaming chariot.

Another myth explained the yearly flooding of the Nile, the main river that flows through Egypt. Its rising waters were said to be the tears of the mother goddess, Isis. She was weeping for her husband, Osiris, who had been murdered by their jealous brother, Seth.

Sekhmet was a powerful goddess with a woman's body and a lion's head. The god Re sent her to punish humans after they stopped worshiping him.

The Egyptians also believed in a mythical, catlike creature that they called the Sphinx. It had the body of a lion and a man's head.

The Sphinx was the protector of the Egyptian rulers, or pharaohs. It was also an incarnation of Horus, the god of the sky, who guided dead souls on their journey to the Underworld.

Catwoman
Batman's feline foe, Catwoman, is a skillful thief who wears a catsuit. She is not fighting for the forces of evil—she is simply out to steal whatever she can get her claws on!

The Sphinx stands in front of the Great Pyramids of Giza in Egypt.

American myths

Serpent symbol
Superman took his emblem from a design on an ancient blanket that had been made by the Iroquois. The "S" shape represented the snake spirit, which had the power to heal.

There were hundreds of different native North American peoples, each with its own myths. Many of these stories tell of supernatural powers that lived in the natural world—in the Earth itself, in animals, or even in the weather. These powers acted as guardian spirits, or totems, who helped and protected humans.

Some North Americans carved tall totem poles using the shapes of their guardian spirits.

One figure was the Thunderbird—an enormous eagle that was the god of thunder, lightning, and fire.

There are many different creator-gods. The Ute people said that Manitou was the Great Spirit who created the mountains and all the animals. He made the birds by tossing a handful of leaves into the air—each leaf became a bird!

You have now read about many myths and tales from all around the world. See what other stories you can unearth and find out what other gods, goddesses, heroes, and monsters appear in these tales.

A brightly colored totem pole that was carved by the Kwakiutl people, who lived in the Pacific Northwest. It is topped with an eagle, complete with outstretched wings.

Change of heart
At first, Manitou Raven was on the side of the evil Atlantean priestess Gamemnae. However, he switched sides to the Justice League after seeing the bravery of the Green Lantern.

Glossary

Avenge
To pay someone back for their evil behavior.

Condemn
To judge and punish a person.

Constellation
A group of stars that seem, when seen from the Earth, to make a pattern in the night sky.

Cosmos
The whole of the universe.

Deity
Another name for a god or goddess.

Dethrone
To remove a king or queen from power.

Exile
When a person is forced to spend time away from their home.

Feline
Describes behavior or appearance that is like a cat.

Forge
To make something out of metal by heating it and shaping it, or a very hot fire in which metal is heated until it is so hot it can be shaped.

Foundry
A place for metalworking.

Girdle
A belt or sash that is worn around the waist of a woman.

Hybrid
A mixture, made partly of one thing and partly of another.

Immortal
A being, such as a god, that will never die.

Incarnation
Appearing in physical, bodily form.

Mortal
A being, such as a human, that will live for a limited time and then die.

Mythology
A collection of stories that tells about magical beings from an earlier age.

Nymph
In Greek mythology, a beautiful maiden who usually had one parent who was a god.

Pantheon
A collection of gods. The Greek and Roman pantheons contain very similar gods, but with different names.

Regal
Describes behavior fitting for a king or queen.

Sorceress
Another word for a witch.

Supernatural
Something magical or spiritual that is beyond the laws of nature.

Telepathically
Communicating with another person or animal from mind to mind, without words.

Totem
An animal or object that represents a divine spirit.

Index